Published in 2023 by Orange Mosquito
An Imprint of Welbeck Children's Limited
part of Welbeck Publishing Group.
Based in London and Sydney.
www.welbeckpublishing.com

In collaboration with Mosquito Books Barcelona S.L.

© Mosquito Books Barcelona, SL 2022
Text © Francesca Ferretti de Blonay 2022
Illustration © Carmen Casado 2022
Translation: Laura McGloughlin
Publisher: Margaux Durigon
Production: Jess Brisley

ISBN: 9781914519741
eISBN: 9781914519758

Printed in China
10 9 8 7 6 5 4 3 2 1

FSC
www.fsc.org
MIX
Paper | Supporting
responsible forestry
FSC® C020056

Francesca Ferretti de Blonay · Carmen Casado

JOHN LENNON & YOKO ONO

ORANGE
M·O·S·Q·U·I·T·O

ENGLAND

England was invaded by a wave of change. Pop culture, created by and for young people, promoted pleasure and modernity.

WHERE?

While the Beatles were releasing their first song *"Love Me Do"* in Liverpool, the Rolling Stones were giving their first concert in London. All this was happening in 1962.

the MARQUEE bar & club

POP CULTURE

Europe discovered the American way of life, with its entertainment, music, and fashion. A wind of freedom was blowing through the world of arts. Personified by the Beatles, rock found its audience: Beatlemania had begun!

ROCK 'N' ROLL

Rock 'n' roll made its appearance on the European stage with the guitarist and singer Chuck Berry. It had an unprecedented impact on young people all over the world. The English-speaking pop-rock movement was unstoppable!

WHEN?

Yoko Ono and John Lennon met on November 9th, 1966, during an exhibition of Yoko's work at Indica Gallery in London. She was 33 and an acclaimed artist. He was 26 and one of the four uber-famous Beatles!

1960S REVOLUTION!

May '68

In Paris, students demanded greater freedoms, taking to the streets and throwing cobblestones and setting up barricades to demonstrate their frustrations against Western capitalism and outdated education systems. The protests ended in battles and echoed the spirit of the French Revolution of 1789.

Nixon

President of the United States, Richard Nixon, pressed ahead with the Vietnam War, despite numerous protests in favor of peace.

Woodstock

At Woodstock Festival (1969), a symbol of hippie culture, there were 32 gigs by folk, rock, soul, and blues groups … and a crowd of 500,000!

3 DAYS of PEACE & MUSIC

Hippie Culture

Born in the United States, the hippie movement spread to the rest of the world. Under the banner of freedom, it significantly influenced music, fashion, and society in general.

Youth in Power

Young people became a source of inspiration for English and Parisian fashion brands. High-end fashion labels opened their first ready-to-wear shops!

The Rolling Stones

British rock group founded in 1962 by Brian Jones, Ian Stewart, Mick Jagger, Keith Richards, Bill Wyman, and Charlie Watts. Their first big hit, "Satisfaction," took the world by storm!

The Moon landing:

In July 1969, millions of people watched two U.S. astronauts walk on the moon: Neil Armstrong and Edwin "Buzz" Aldrin.

YOKO

Yoko Ono was born on February 18th, 1933, in Tokyo. From an aristocratic Japanese family, she led a privileged life until the day World War II broke out. She admitted that the deprivation of war forged her strength of character. At the age of 14, she was a brilliant, rebellious girl predestined for making ground-breaking art.

AVANT-GARDE

Like all avant-garde artists, Yoko settled in Greenwich Village, the cultural heart of New York City. She took part in concert-exhibitions and developed an extraordinary form of art. Her early works were happenings, spontaneous artistic events which explored the everyday.

PERFORMER

Her work was ever more daring. Yoko became a true performance artist. Her artistic performances used poetry and theater and invited interaction from the observer. Yoko's pieces were brief, but powerful. In 1966, her work was shown in Indica Gallery, where she met John Lennon.

BACKGROUND

It was a heady time in which artists expressed themselves in unusual ways! Yoko Ono presented her ideas through original poetic and philosophical performances. Her works of art directly addressed the public. In them she threw out all kinds of instructions, like "*Breathe*," to stimulate thought and to open up consciousness.

APPLE

BREATH

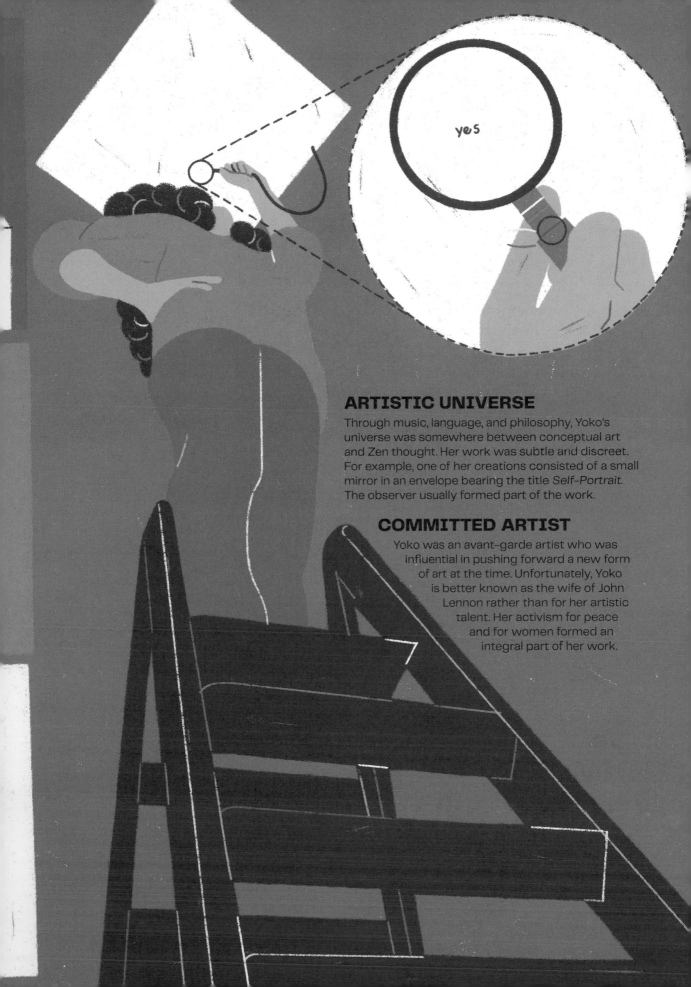

ARTISTIC UNIVERSE

Through music, language, and philosophy, Yoko's universe was somewhere between conceptual art and Zen thought. Her work was subtle and discreet. For example, one of her creations consisted of a small mirror in an envelope bearing the title *Self-Portrait*. The observer usually formed part of the work.

COMMITTED ARTIST

Yoko was an avant-garde artist who was influential in pushing forward a new form of art at the time. Unfortunately, Yoko is better known as the wife of John Lennon rather than for her artistic talent. Her activism for peace and for women formed an integral part of her work.

THEMES

The meaning of life, peace

Yoko Ono chose to convey a lot by saying very little. She especially loved haiku. These short Japanese poems without rhyme or punctuation usually speak of nature or reality perceived by the senses, and the aim is to communicate an idea using the fewest possible number of words.

In 1962 Yoko Ono published *Grapefruit*, a collection of instructions for making musical compositions, paintings, and different acts of everyday life. One example was how to make minimalist sculptures using simple objects, like an apple placed on a plexiglass pedestal with the inscription "Apple." The idea of the piece of art, represented by the object and its designated name, was more important than the object itself. In this vein, the apple can be seen from a different perspective, rich in new meaning. Yoko transformed everyday objects, taking them out of context.

JOHN

John Lennon was born during World War II on October 9th, 1940. There was no work in Liverpool, and little John's parents struggled to take care of him properly. Eventually, he went to live with his aunt Mimi in Woolton (Liverpool), where he grew up surrounded by his cousins.

THE MUSIC

With a grandfather who was a singer and a father who dreamed of being one, music was a huge part of John's heritage and who he was. In 1956, his mother bought him his first guitar, a cheap Gallotone. At the age of 17, John heard Elvis Presley on the radio and from then on he became obsessed with rock 'n' roll.

ROCK 'N' ROLL

Fascinated and inspired by the music of Chuck Berry, John founded his first group, The Quarrymen. At one of the band's local concerts, John met Paul McCartney, and he asked him to join his band. Paul was 15 years old and John was 17!

Seven years later, the song "Love Me Do" was a smash hit and established the Beatles: John Lennon, Paul McCartney, George Harrison, and Ringo Starr, as serious musicians.

The Beatles had to work hard before becoming successful. Despite the tragic death of John's mother just before his 18th birthday, which plunged him into a deep sadness, the group continued to rise in the charts. The fans were out of control; young women fainted when they saw the "Fab Four." Beatlemania was at its peak!

BACKGROUND

Like many other young people of his time, John's childhood sufferings had a profound effect on him. He was an extremely sensitive man who could fly into terrible rages. Music served as a refuge, as he sought to free himself from the past. Deep down he was searching for peace—the peace he sang about and so inwardly needed. Music was his life.

A FREE SPIRIT

John's personality, humor, and devil–may–care attitude set him apart. Above all, despite his sarcastic wisecracks, he was an artist full of imagination and deep sincerity.

THEMES

Love, non-violence, the rights of man and woman

John scribbled some words on a blank page: "*All you need is love.*" It sounded great, and what's more, it was true! Far from a feeble message, the songwriter was posing questions about the violence that resides in the human being.

His songs were of their time but also timeless because they addressed the depths of being human. Simplicity and profundity made his hits true anthems. John condemned violence of all kinds, from the Vietnam War to the student barricades in Paris. As his song "*Power to the People*" revealed, he defended the rights of man and woman, while recognizing that he himself hadn't always treated the women in his life well. He also spoke about his love for his mother, to whom he dedicated touching songs like "*Julia*" and "*Mother.*"

FIRST CONTACT

At Indica Gallery in London, Yoko Ono was doing the final preparations for her latest exhibition when John Lennon visited the hall before the opening. There he discovered a universe that echoed his and he was totally enchanted; it was spiritual and artistic love at first sight.

UNION

Almost two years later, after that initial contact, John invited Yoko to his home. They started an affair and during this time they recorded their first single together, titled "*Unfinished Music No. 1: Two Virgins*" John and Yoko posed naked for the picture on the record sleeve! Puritan England was horrified! In 1969, John and Yoko were married in Gibraltar.

ADMIRATION

In Yoko, John had found the woman of his dreams, a life and creative companion. For both of them, their mutual love had truly transformed their perception of life. This feeling would become a love for the whole world, in the form of a call for peace.

HAIR PEACE.

CREATIONS

During their honeymoon, Yoko and John settled in Amsterdam's Hilton Hotel and created the *Bed–In* for Peace event in protest against the Vietnam War. Images of the couple in pajamas in bed went all over the world. A second Bed–In took place in Montreal, where John composed an anthem for peace: "*Give Peace a Chance.*" After these events, Yoko brought out her first solo album and John left the Beatles.

Harassed by the media, the couple left London for New York City and settled in Manhattan in the Dakota Building. There, John found something resembling freedom: finally, he could walk around without being accosted by fans. Later, John said that Yoko had been unfairly blamed for him leaving the Beatles, and that she had saved him by showing him a more authentic perspective on life.

COMMITTED LOVE

Their mutual commitment to each other also extended to the whole world, symbolized by the bed, the cradle of their love, and offered by both artists in service of world peace.

imag

FUSION

Thanks to their activism for peace, Yoko and John became one of the most high-profile couples in the world. Their artistic collaboration continued to bear fruit and in 1971, John brought out the album *Imagine*. It was an instant success! "Imagine" is also the title of one of the most iconic songs of John Lennon's solo career. It is an anthem for peace which invites the listener to imagine a world without borders, without nations, without religion, without reasons to kill, and without possessions. A world where everyone is united in a brotherhood of man; an ideology bearing the characteristic Ono-Lennon stamp.

After some time, Yoko and John's euphoric love began to diminish and John's internal unease returned. The Beatles had broken up, after ten years together in joy and in sorrow. Now John was tormented by fears about his romantic fusion with Yoko, and he began to make all sorts of mistakes, putting his marriage at risk.

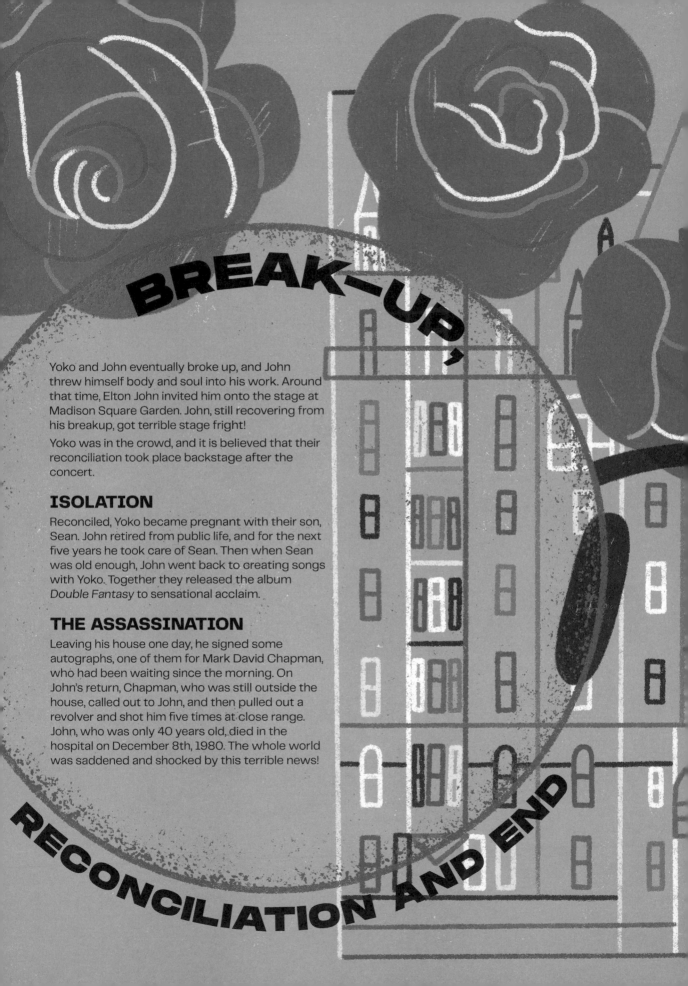

BREAK-UP, RECONCILIATION AND END

Yoko and John eventually broke up, and John threw himself body and soul into his work. Around that time, Elton John invited him onto the stage at Madison Square Garden. John, still recovering from his breakup, got terrible stage fright!

Yoko was in the crowd, and it is believed that their reconciliation took place backstage after the concert.

ISOLATION

Reconciled, Yoko became pregnant with their son, Sean. John retired from public life, and for the next five years he took care of Sean. Then when Sean was old enough, John went back to creating songs with Yoko. Together they released the album *Double Fantasy* to sensational acclaim.

THE ASSASSINATION

Leaving his house one day, he signed some autographs, one of them for Mark David Chapman, who had been waiting since the morning. On John's return, Chapman, who was still outside the house, called out to John, and then pulled out a revolver and shot him five times at close range. John, who was only 40 years old, died in the hospital on December 8th, 1980. The whole world was saddened and shocked by this terrible news!

How could a couple like John and Yoko not be remembered! Their story, full of love, activism, and drama, shaped the 1970s. John was a Beatle and Yoko an avant-garde artist, but together they became an iconic couple of the pacifist movement, representatives of peace and love.

INSPIRATION

Some artists like Lady Gaga claim to have been inspired by the couple's commitment to peace. This is what drove her to create her own foundation to help those most in need in 2011. Other artists have done the same.

IMMORTALS

Like many other geniuses, John Lennon shaped the world of music forever.
As for Yoko Ono, a female avant-garde artist phenomenon, she is a living reminder of the story of the 1960s and the formidable creative energy that ruled that era.

FAMOUS QUOTES

Yoko Ono

Every drop in the ocean counts.

The regret of my life is that I have not said
"I love you" often enough.

Art is my life and my life is art.

Only art and music have the power to bring peace.

You may think I'm small, but I have a universe in my mind.

FAMOUS QUOTES

John Lennon

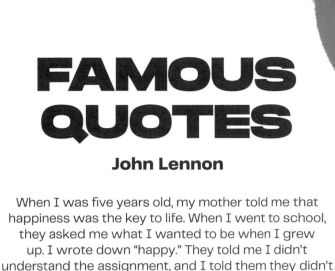

When I was five years old, my mother told me that happiness was the key to life. When I went to school, they asked me what I wanted to be when I grew up. I wrote down "happy." They told me I didn't understand the assignment, and I told them they didn't understand life.

Time you enjoy wasting was not time wasted.

It all exists, even if it's in your mind.

A dream you dream alone is only a dream.
A dream you dream together is reality.

If everyone demanded peace instead of another television set, then there'd be peace.

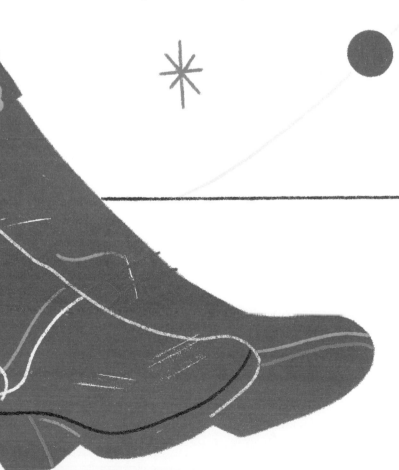

WISH TREE

A WORK BY YOKO ONO

This piece has been recreated all over the world. It is inspired by Yoko's childhood in Japan where she would contemplate trees covered in prayers that swirled in the wind like thousands of white flowers. In 1996, Yoko Ono invited the observer to write a wish on a scrap of paper and hang it from a tree. Her idea – originally dating back to 1981– was that in writing our deepest desires, we can contribute to creating a better world. It is as though we are offering something of ourselves to the world. A simple but tremendously symbolic act

Over a million messages have been written and collected for the Wish Tree. Different versions of Wish Tree can be found in places like the Guggenheim Museum in Bilbao, the Museum of Contemporary Art in Tokyo, the Hirshhorn Museum and Sculpture Garden in Washington, and the Guggenheim Museum in Venice.

Themes: peace, imagination, the crowd, creative energy, the universe.

Technique: paper, string, participatory writing, tree.

ALL YOU NEED IS LOVE

A WORK BY JOHN LENNON

In 1967, the Beatles' manager announced that the group had been chosen to represent Great Britain on a television program, the first of which would be broadcast live all over the world. John was ready for the challenge.

Composed in 15 days, the song "*All You Need is Love*" was written to send out a powerful message to the whole world. The first notes of the song were a reproduction of the Marseillaise, the French national anthem, but instead of calling the people to arms, Lennon's song defended love. As the voices came in after the first few notes, the word "love" was repeated three times: "*Love, love, love.*"

Across the planet, in the middle of the Vietnam War, the song rose to the top of the charts and became a point of reference. It was considered an anthem for the hippie movement, whose ideology was one of non-violence.

In 2009, the song was performed simultaneously in 156 countries in the context of the fight against AIDS in Africa.

Themes: the ideal of love, peace and unity, the anti-war, countercultural movement.

MARCEL DUCHAMP

French-American artist, anarchist, symbol of New York City's Greenwich Village, and friend of Yoko Ono.

Member of the Beatles from the age of 15, he impressed John with his musical talent. The two artists always signed their songs together.

PAUL McCARTNEY

ARTISTS

CYNTHIA POWELL

John's first wife and mother of his first son Julian. Cynthia was with John in the early days of the Beatles.

BOB DYLAN

The famous singer had a positive effect on Lennon's lyrics, which became more personal and poetic.

He discovered the Beatles when they were only known in Liverpool. He became their manager and contributed to their growing international fame.

American artist, gallery owner, and editor, he was the founder of Fluxus, a community which brought avant-garde artists like Yoko Ono and the composer John Cage together.

BRIAN EPSTEIN

GEORGE MACIUNAS

AND FRIENDS

THE ROLLING STONES

Although they were chart rivals, the Beatles and the Stones thought highly of each other.

GLOSSARY

Activism: an action to make a change or stop a change in society. An activist is someone who wants to make the world a better place and can be writers, artists, scientists, teachers, community leaders …

AIDS: a term that stands for "Acquired Immunodeficiency Syndrome". It is the most advanced stage of HIV ("Human Immunodeficiency Virus") which is a virus that attacks the body's immune system.

Avant-garde: a term describing people or works that are experimental, bold or innovative.

Capitalism: a system based on citizens, not governments, owning and running companies.

Chuck Berry: an American guitarist, singer and songwriter who pioneered rock and roll music. He is considered as a major influence on 20th century popular music.

Conceptual art: a style of art where the concepts or ideas in the work are more important than traditional aesthetic and the finished object.

Hippie culture: a movement focusing on nonviolence and love. It promotes openness and tolerance, preferring to avoid materialism, money and politics.

Puritan: a person who practices or preaches a stricter moral code than is generally followed.

Vietnam war: a long conflict fought between communist North Vietnam and the government of Southern Vietnam, and its main ally, the United States. It started in 1955 and ended in 1975.